LET'S FIND OUT ABOUT

Jewish Synagogues

Mandy Ross

www.raintreepublishers.co.uk
Visit our website to find out more information about Raintree books.

To order:
☎ Phone 44 (0) 1865 888112
🖨 Send a fax to 44 (0) 1865 314091
💻 Visit the Raintree Bookshop at www.raintreepublishers.co.uk to browse our catalogue and order online.

First published in Great Britain by Raintree, Halley Court, Jordan Hill, Oxford, OX2 8EJ, part of Harcourt Education.
Raintree is a registered trademark of Harcourt Education Ltd.

© Harcourt Education Ltd 2006.
First published in paperback in 2007.
The moral right of the proprietor has been asserted.

Editorial: Daniel Nunn and Sarah Chappelow
Design: Ron Kamen and Philippa Baile
Picture research: Hannah Taylor and Sally Claxton
Production: Duncan Gilbert
Religious consultant: Susannah Alexander, Education Officer at the Jewish Museum, London

Originated by Modern Age
Printed and bound in China by WKT

ISBN 10: 1 844 21139 8 (hardback)
ISBN 13: 978 1 844 21139 5 (hardback)
10 09 08 07 06
10 9 8 7 6 5 4 3 2 1

ISBN 10: 1 844 21146 0 (paperback)
ISBN 13: 978 1 844 21146 3 (paperback)
11 10 09 08 07 06
10 9 8 7 6 5 4 3 2 1

British Library Cataloguing in Publication Data
Ross, Mandy
  Let's find out about Jewish synagogues
  1. Synagogues – Juvenile literature
  2. Judaism – Customs and practices – Juvenile literature
  I. Title II. Jewish synagogues
  296.6'5
A full catalogue record for this book is available from the British Library.

Acknowledgements
The publishers would like to thank the following for permission to reproduce photographs:

Alamy pp. **9** (Hisham Ibrahim/Photov.com), **12** (Helene Rogers), **13 bottom** (Israelimages/Mike Ganor), **20** (Israelimages/Richard Nowitz); Chris Schwarz p. **18**; Corbis pp. **4** (Wolfgang Kaehler), **5** (Ted Spiegel), **7** (Hanan Isachar), **8** (David H. Wells), **13 top** (Ted Spiegel), **16 bottom** (Alain Keler), **19** (David H. Wells), **21** (Denis Degnan), **22** (Paul A. Souders), **24** (Najilah Feanny), **26 bottom** (Macduff Everton), **27** (Farrell Graham); Getty Images pp. **16 top** (Photodisc), **25** (Photodisc); Impact Photos p. **17**; Manchester Jewish Museum p. **26 top**; Rabbi Mark Goldsmith and the Finchley Progressive Synagogue pp. **14**, **23**; Trip pp. **6** (Itzhak Genut), **10** (Helene Rogers), **11**, **15**.

Cover photograph of the Old Synagogue in Port Elizabeth, South Africa, reproduced with permission of Corbis/Luc Hosten/Gallo Images.

Every effort has been made to contact copyright holders of any material reproduced in this book. Any omissions will be rectified in subsequent printings if notice is given to the publishers.

The paper used to print this book comes from sustainable resources.

Contents

Words appearing in the text in bold, **like this**, are explained in the Glossary. The Jewish words used in this book are listed with a pronunciation guide on page 29.

What is a synagogue?

A synagogue is a building where Jewish people go to pray, meet, and learn. Some synagogues are beautiful, grand buildings. Others are simple, small buildings or even houses.

Jewish people meet at the synagogue to pray on **Shabbat**, the Jewish day of rest. Shabbat lasts from sunset on Friday to sunset on Saturday. Jewish people also meet at the synagogue for **festivals** and for special days such as weddings.

This is the Great Synagogue in Budapest, Hungary. The writing over the door is in Hebrew.

The synagogue is a busy place during the week, too. There may be youth clubs, toddlers' play groups, and lunches for older people. The **rabbi** and volunteers often work in the local neighbourhood, helping people to feel they are part of a **community**.

Inside a large, modern synagogue in Seattle, in the United States. The rabbi is leading the service from the front.

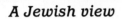

A Jewish view

Our synagogue here in Birmingham was built over 60 years ago. I love it best when the synagogue is full of people, old and young, coming together to celebrate a special day in the Jewish calendar.
Rabbi Margaret Jacobi, a rabbi in Birmingham, in the United Kingdom

Jews and Judaism

Judaism is the religion followed by Jewish people. Jewish people pray to one God. Their **holy** book is called the **Hebrew Bible**. Jewish people believe that their Bible shows them how God wants them to live a good life.

Judaism teaches how to pray to God, and how to treat other people. It also teaches how to mark important times in life, such as the birth of a new baby, growing up, marriage, or death. Jewish people say special prayers at each of these times.

These Jews are welcoming a new baby into the Jewish community.

Did you know Judaism started about 4,000 years ago. Judaism, Christianity, and Islam all share the same beginnings and some of the same stories and beliefs.

This ruined synagogue in Israel was built more than 2,300 years ago.

Judaism is one of the oldest religions in the world. However, there are only about thirteen million Jewish people in the world. This is far fewer than many other religions.

There are lots of different kinds of Judaism. Some are more traditional and strict than others. Many synagogues reflect these differences.

Synagogue buildings

Synagogues have been built in many different styles over the years and around the world. Often they look like other places of **worship** in the country where they are built. So some synagogues, like the one shown on page 4, look a little like a church, with grand doors and windows. Others are built in the style of a **mosque**, with beautiful domes and round arches.

The Great Synagogue in Florence, Italy (below), has a beautiful dome made of copper.

Did you know

One of the oldest synagogues in the world is in Jerusalem. It is called the Tomb of David and was built in about 75 CE . It may have been built first as a church by early Christians.

Some synagogues are quite plain outside but look more interesting inside. Many have beautiful decorations, such as candles, coloured tiles, or **Hebrew** writings on the wall.

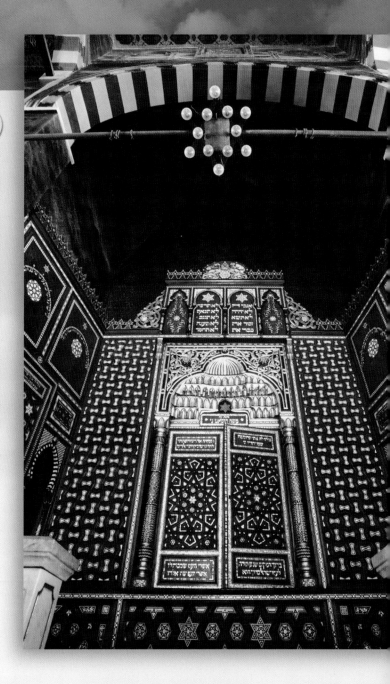

This is the Ben Ezra Synagogue in Cairo, Egypt. It is richly decorated inside.

Inside the Synagogue

Synagogue services are led by the **rabbi**. The rabbi is a teacher and Jewish leader. The rabbi stands on a raised platform called the **bimah**. In traditional synagogues, the bimah is in the middle of the synagogue. In other synagogues, the bimah is at the front. All the seats face the bimah.

Every synagogue has a special cupboard called the **Ark**, which holds the **Torah scrolls**. The Ark always faces in the direction of Jerusalem, the most **holy** place for Jewish people. So when people pray towards the Ark, they look towards Jerusalem.

This woman rabbi is reading from the Torah scroll.

This is the Ark at Bevis Marks Synagogue in London, in the United Kingdom.

This diagram shows the layout of a typical traditional synagogue.

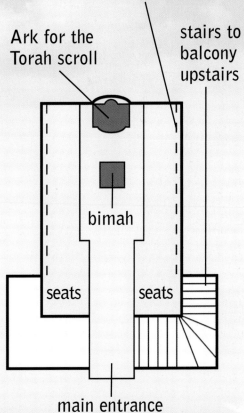

decorated windows

Ark for the Torah scroll

stairs to balcony upstairs

bimah

seats

seats

main entrance

In traditional synagogues, men and women sit in separate areas. The women may sit upstairs, on the balcony. But in many other synagogues, families sit together during services.

Some synagogues are beautifully decorated inside, with arches and colourful details. Others are quite simple and plain. Many synagogues have beautiful windows with coloured glass. These show Jewish symbols or stories from the Torah.

Things to see

When the **Ark** is opened, you can see the **Torah scroll** inside. Torah scrolls have beautiful covers made of wood, or cloth **embroidered** with gold or silver.

Above the Ark there is a lamp that is always kept lit. This is called the Ner Tamid, or everlasting light. It is a symbol of God's everlasting love.

These are Torah scrolls inside an Ark. The bells, called rimonim, tinkle as they are taken out.

Did you know

Torah scrolls are very precious because Jews believe they contain God's teachings. When someone reads from the scrolls, they use a pointer so they do not touch the writing.

The Ner Tamid on the left is in front of a Star of David.

This stained-glass window at the Jerusalem Central Synagogue celebrates the Jewish New Year.

You may also see other Jewish symbols, such as a seven-branched candlestick. Another Jewish symbol is a six-pointed star. This is known as the Star of David.

Many synagogues show God's most important laws, the Ten Commandments. The Ten Commandments tell how to live without doing wrong, such as killing or stealing.

Worshipping at a synagogue

There are **Shabbat** services at most synagogues every week. Some synagogues hold services every day. Most prayers are said in **Hebrew**. Some prayers are sung to beautiful tunes that are hundreds or even thousands of years old.

A Jewish view

I like going to synagogue on Shabbat to be with other Jewish people, because I'm the only Jewish boy at my school. It makes me feel more Jewish.

Josh, age twelve, from Birmingham in the United Kingdom

These families are worshipping together at a modern synagogue service.

Every week, during the Shabbat service, the **Torah scroll** is taken out of the **Ark**. Then the **rabbi** or members of the synagogue read aloud from it in Hebrew.

Usually the rabbi gives a special talk called a sermon. In the sermon, the rabbi explains Jewish teachings and how they can help people to live a good life. After the service, everyone says **blessings** together called Kiddush before drinking a little wine and sharing bread.

During the Shabbat service, the Torah scroll is carried around the synagogue so that everyone can see it.

Showing respect

During synagogue services, everyone dresses in neat, clean clothes to show respect for God. Boys and men cover their heads with a hat or a small cap called a kippah, or yarmulke. Jewish men and older boys may wear a prayer **shawl** called a tallith.

Did you know

A tallith is a white, rectangle-shaped shawl made of wool, linen, or silk. It has blue or black stripes, and fringes along the edges. The fringes are symbols which help to remind people of God's commandments.

This man is blessing his son under a tallith.

Married women cover their hair with hats or scarves. Some girls and women may wear a kippah and tallith.

Visitors to a synagogue service usually sit quietly to show respect. After the Kiddush **blessings** at the end of the service, they will be invited to sip wine and share bread. Often, there may be cakes and snacks as well.

This woman **rabbi** from a modern synagogue in the United Kingdom is wearing a kippah.

Festivals

As each year passes, Jewish people come to the synagogue to celebrate the **festivals**. Jewish New Year, or Rosh Hashanah, comes in September or October. During the service, a ram's horn called a shofar is blown to welcome the New Year.

Ten days after Rosh Hashanah comes Yom Kippur, the Day of **Atonement**. This is a serious day, when Jewish people say prayers to say sorry for things they have done wrong through the year.

A rabbi blows a shofar to call people to prayer at the New Year.

Succoth is a celebration of the **harvest**. At the synagogue or at home, many Jewish people build a small hut called a succah, decorated with leaves, fruit, and vegetables. They eat their meals there for a week, saying prayers to thank God for the fruit and vegetables that have grown ripe over the summer.

A Jewish view

I love building the succah at synagogue every year at Succoth, and decorating the walls with branches and fruit and flowers. This year a lot of people helped, and we had lots of fun.
Rachel, age fourteen, from New York, in the United States

This succah is in Brooklyn, New York, in the United States.

Special events

The synagogue is always full during special events to mark important times in people's lives. Newborn babies are **blessed** by the **rabbi**. The name is announced and everyone says prayers to welcome the baby.

At the age of thirteen, a Jewish boy may become a bar mitzvah, and at twelve or thirteen, a Jewish girl may become a bat mitzvah. This is the start of being an adult. Family and friends come to the synagogue to hear the bar mitzvah boy or bat mitzvah girl read from the **Torah**.

This girl is reading from the Torah scroll as she becomes a bat mitzvah.

A Jewish view

I felt very nervous before my bat mitzvah, but once I started reading and singing, I really enjoyed being up on the **bimah**.
Sarah, age 22, from New York, in the United States

At Jewish weddings, the bride and bridegroom stand under a **canopy** called a chuppah. The chuppah is a symbol of the home they will make together. They say blessings together and make their marriage promises.

A bride and groom stand under the wedding canopy, or chuppah.

A place to meet

The synagogue is not just a place for **worship**. After school or on Sunday mornings, many synagogues hold classes. In these classes, children learn about Jewish life and customs. There may also be classes for adults who want to learn more about **Judaism** or how to speak **Hebrew**.

A Jewish view

I go to classes at my synagogue on Sunday mornings. I like learning the Hebrew letters so that I can read in Hebrew, and I like it when we read stories from the Bible, like Jonah and the whale.

Joe, age five, from Birmingham in the United Kingdom

This girl is learning Hebrew at a synagogue in Belfast, in the United Kingdom.

Synagogues are also places where people can have fun! These children are celebrating at a party for Hanukkah (see page 25).

Many synagogues hold social events so that people can get to know one another. The **rabbi** and other members of the synagogue visit and look after people who cannot get out of their homes because they are ill or elderly.

Some synagogues also have links with people of other religions who live in the neighbourhood. Jewish people may meet with members of their local church, **mosque**, or temple to learn about each others' religion and **community**.

Worshipping at home

Jewish people can **worship** anywhere, not just at the synagogue. Many important parts of Jewish worship take place at home.

On Friday evenings, Jewish people light candles at home to welcome **Shabbat**. Shabbat is a day of rest when no one goes to work.

This girl is lighting candles at home to welcome Shabbat.

Did you know

At Passover, Jewish people eat flat crackers called matzo instead of bread. This is to remember how their ancestors had to escape so quickly there was no time to bake proper bread!

This plate shows some of the special foods eaten at Passover.

At Passover, in the spring, family and friends are invited to a special meal called the seder. There they eat special foods to remember Jewish people who escaped from slavery long ago.

Hanukkah is celebrated in the winter. Jewish people light candles every night for eight nights. This is to remember a time more than 2,000 years ago when they won back their freedom to worship. Children are given presents or money for Hanukkah.

Synagogues around the world

The upper windows of this 19th-century synagogue building in Manchester, in the United Kingdom, have round arches like the arches in the Santa Maria la Blanca (below).

Some synagogues are very famous. The synagogue of Santa Maria la Blanca in Toledo, Spain, was built about 800 years ago. It has round arches in the style of a **mosque**. Later, in the 16th century, the building was turned into a church.

The round arches of the Santa Maria la Blanca synagogue are decorated with fancy patterns.

Beth Shalom Synagogue, in Pennsylvania in the United States, was designed by a famous architect called Frank Lloyd Wright. Its high roof is made of glass. The building is designed in the shape of a mountain. This is a symbol of Mount Sinai in Egypt. The **Hebrew Bible** tells how Moses climbed Mount Sinai to talk to God.

The glass roof of the Beth Shalom Synagogue glows in the dark when the lights are lit inside.

Judaism around the world

Judaism began about 4,000 years ago in the area now called Israel. Since then, Jewish people have settled all over the world. Today there are about thirteen million Jews.

Judaism is a very small religion. For every 500 people in the world, just one of them is Jewish. The greatest number of Jewish people live in the United States and in Israel. There are also large Jewish **communities** in France, Russia, Ukraine, Canada, and the United Kingdom.

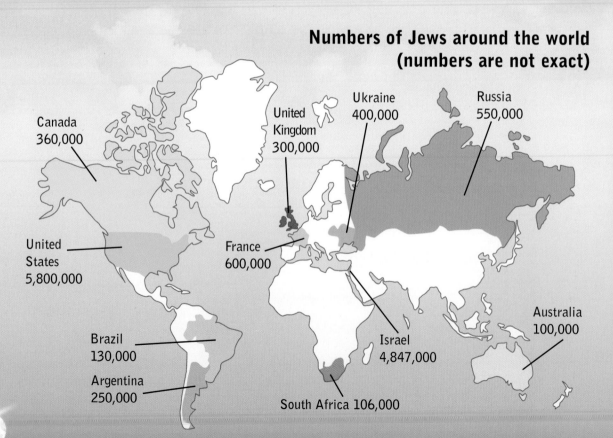

Numbers of Jews around the world (numbers are not exact)

Canada 360,000

United Kingdom 300,000

Ukraine 400,000

Russia 550,000

United States 5,800,000

France 600,000

Brazil 130,000

Argentina 250,000

Israel 4,847,000

South Africa 106,000

Australia 100,000

Jewish words

These are Jewish words that have been used in this book. You can find out how to say them by reading the pronunciation guide in brackets after each word.

bar mitzvah [bar mitz-vah] – when a boy reads from the Torah scroll, marking the beginning of his adult life

bat mitzvah [bat mitz-vah] – when a girl reads from the Torah scroll, marking the beginning of her adult life

bimah [bi-mah] – the platform where the rabbi stands to lead a service in the synagogue

chuppah [hup-ah] – the canopy that the bride and groom stand under when they get married

Hanukkah [han-u-ka] – the festival of lights

Kiddush [kidd-ush] – blessings said over bread and wine

kippah [ki-pah] – a skull cap, worn to show respect for God. It is also known as a yarmulke.

matzo [matz-ah] – flat bread or crackers eaten at Passover

Ner Tamid [nair ta-meed] – a lamp above the Ark that is always kept lit

rabbi [rab-eye] – a Jewish teacher or leader

rimonim [rim-on-eem] – the tiny bells that decorate the handles of the Torah scroll

Rosh Hashanah [rosh ha-shan-ah] – Jewish New Year

seder [say-der] – a special meal during which the story of the Passover is told

Shabbat [sha-bat] – the seventh day of the week and the Jewish day of rest. Shabbat lasts from sunset on Friday to sunset on Saturday.

succah [suk-ah] – a little outdoor booth or hut decorated with fruits and vegetables, where Jewish people eat their meals during Succoth

Succoth [suk-ot] – the harvest festival

synagogue [sin-a-gog] – the Jewish place of worship

tallith [tal-eet] – a prayer shawl

Torah [tor-ah] – the first five books of the Hebrew Bible, which are written on the scroll

Yom Kippur [yom kee-pur] – the day of atonement

Glossary

Ark special cupboard in a synagogue where the Torah scrolls are kept

atonement feeling and saying sorry for things you have done wrong

bimah platform where the rabbi stands to lead a service in the synagogue

bless ask God to watch over someone or something

canopy roof made of cloth

community group of people with a shared sense of belonging

embroider to decorate cloth with stitching

festival a time of celebration

harvest bringing in the crops at the end of the summer

Hebrew the traditional language of Jewish prayer

Hebrew Bible the Jewish holy book. It is almost the same as the Christian Old Testament.

holy to do with God

Judaism the religion followed by Jewish people

mosque a Muslim place of worship

rabbi a Jewish teacher or leader

scroll collection of writings written in one very long strip, which is wrapped around two wooden end-pieces.

Shabbat the seventh day of the week and the Jewish day of rest. It lasts from sunset on Friday to sunset on Saturday.

shawl a large piece of cloth worn to cover the head or shoulders

Torah the first five books of the Hebrew Bible, which are written on the scroll

worship to pray to God

Finding out more

Visiting a synagogue

Jewish people welcome visitors to their synagogues, as long as they behave respectfully. Visitors should dress sensibly, in long sleeved tops and long trousers (or long skirts for girls). When they arrive at the synagogue, boys and men will be asked to cover their heads with a hat or a cap. In traditional synagogues, girls and women will be expected to sit separately from boys and men.

In some synagogues, people may be allowed to take photographs, but they should always ask permission first.

More books to read

Celebrations: Hanukkah, Mandy Ross (Heinemann Library, 2001)

Holy Places: The Western Wall, Mandy Ross (Heinemann Library, 2002)

Religions of the World: Judaism, Sue Penney (Heinemann Library, 2002)

Useful websites

http://www.bbc.co.uk/religion/religions/judaism/index.shtml
This website from the BBC looks at all aspects of Judaism.

http://www.judaism.about.com
An information site giving lots of information about Judaism.

Disclaimer

All the Internet addresses (URLs) given in this book were valid at the time of going to press. However, due to the dynamic nature of the Internet, some addresses may have changed, or sites may have ceased to exist since publication. While the author and publishers regret any inconvenience this may cause readers, no responsibility for any such changes can be accepted by either the author or the publishers.

Index